The Prayer Eagle

Dr. D. K. Olukoya

The Prayer Eagle

Published - May 2001
Reprinted - June 2011

ISBN 978-35755-3-8

322, Herbert Macaulay Way,
Yaba P. O. Box 12272, Ikeja, Lagos
Website: www.battlecryng.com
Email: sales@battlecryng.com
Phone: 2348033044239, 01-8044415

I salute my wonderful wife, Pastor Shade, for her invaluable support in the ministry.

I appreciate her unquantifiable support in the book ministry as the cover designer, art editor and art adviser

All Scripture quotation is from the King James Version of the Bible

All rights reserved.
We prohibit reproduction in whole or part without written permission.

The Prayer Eagle

Isaiah 40-27-31: Why sayest thou, O Jacob, and speakest, O Israel, My way is hid from the LORD, and my judgement is passed over from my God? ²⁸Hast thou not known? hast thou not heard, that the everlasting God, the LORD, the Creator of the ends of the earth, fainteth not, neither is weary? There is no searching of his understanding. ²⁹ He giveth power to the faint; and to them that have no might he increaseth strength. ³⁰Even the youths shall faint and be weary, and the young men shall utterly fall:³¹ But they that wait upon the LORD shall renew their strength; they shall mount up with wings as eagles; they shall run, and not be weary; and they shall walk, and not faint.

In the above passage, God was simply asking Jacob why he was complaining; "why are you saying all that you are saying? What are you thinking in your heart? Why are you saying that my face is hid from you? Why are you saying that your rights have been denied you?"

Verse 28 here is speaking of the power and greatness of God.

Have you not known or heard that the Lord, the Creator of the ends of the earth fainteth not, neither is He weary?

Now, for the first time, we know the problems of Jacob. He was complaining; "Why am I going through all these problems? And God answered and said, "it's a pity, so you have not heard that there is no searching of the understanding of the Almighty. But you wait upon Him and your strength shall be renewed, so our problem, Jacob, is that you are weary and fainting, but if you can wait upon the Lord, your strength shall be renewed, and then you will begin to mount up with wings as the eagle."

PRAYERLESSNESS- The bane of our society

One of the major disasters of modern day Christianity is prayerlessness. Prayers cannot be measured like we measure water into the bucket. I have seen men who can pray for ten hours non stop at prayer meetings but immediately they get home from the prayer meeting, they can beat up their wives. I have seen people who can prophesy- "Thus says the Lord" and sometimes, when you look at them, you will think they are not from this planet, that they live in another world, but the same fellow is telling lies.

The Prayer Eagle

There are some people who would say, "I have just completed a 40-day dry fast programme," or" "I have just completed a 21-day dry fast programme," but that same person is an adulterer. I have seen someone who can stand and offer prayers for two hours non-stop, but if an ordinary lizard runs across him or her, he drops the Bible and flee.

There are many churches, where a lot of prayers are going on, but the Lord looks from heaven and says , "This is not praying at all." Many of the things we call prayer mean prayerlessness to God. He calls it 'busy doing nothing'. How would you imagine someone who starts praying now, and immediately, the mind travels to Sokoto; I thank you Lord', the mind is already in Port-Harcourt; 'I want to confess my sins', the mind has travelled to Oyingbo market. And this person may spend the next one hour doing that- just busy doing nothing.

Somebody woke up in the middle of the night and offered prayers. He or she recited seven different Psalms off-heard and prayed fire prayers while standing, but barely the next morning, the same person is engaged in gossips. As far as God is concerned, this fellow is just wasting time. There are many people like that.

Unfortunately, the prayerful churches are not many, nevertheless, everybody is still coming back to pray. Those that are dancing now are coming back to pray. Those who do not hold night vigils now are beginning soon. When the anti-Christ will begin to blow hot airs into people's heads, then many churches will start praying. Very; very soon they will drop disco music and move to pray halls.

Therefore, one of the major disasters that has befallen the modern day Christian is prayerlessness. You may say we pray a lot here at Mountain of Fire and Miracles Ministries - Yes! But at the same time, we have those who are not very serious. They are still doing things that are anti-prayer.

The Prayer Eagle

There is a saying that when a man has not seen other people's father's farms, he would always believe that his own father's farm is the biggest.

I was invited somewhere. It was a Ghanaian fellowship. I spoke the way I normally did and said, "Let us pray." By the time they started, I was shocked. In fact, I had to open my eyes to confirm whether they were really praying. I did not know that what I said was that serious. They prayed like possessed people much so that I found it difficult to stop them even after I had jingled the bell. A minute after the prayers, every person on the front row were sweating profusely, but they were ready to take on the next prayer point.

Again, you may say, compared to other churches, we pray a lot at Mountain of Fire and Miracles yet, the Bible says comparing themselves with themselves, they are not wise. Do not compare your Church with another or compare yourself with another. Rather, compare and weigh yourself with what God wants you to be look at what God has set up and compare yourself with it, and not what somebody else is doing. How can an eagle make friends with a fowl?

If you read through the Acts of the Apostles chapter four, the Bible said that while Apostles prayed, the place they were gathered, shook, and they were all filled with the Holy Ghost, and spoke the word of God with boldness.

Do you know that there are forces that can pick up prayers and swallow them?

I know about a situation like that some years ago. The prayer of some young brothers who prayed in a particular room were not answered until God opened their eyes that somebody had surrounded the whole room with a red thread. They never knew that a wicked power had tied a string round the place. Each time they vowed to hold a vigil, they would find themselves sleeping off at 10:00 p.m. And by the time they realised this, it was morning already.

The Prayer Eagle

When sometimes you want to pray, and you seem uninterested, or it appears as if a power is holding you down, know that some evil powers are around. They do not want you to pray, so they attack the prayer because it is the only thing that bothers them.

There was a time, we were praying here at the Mountain of Fire and Miracles. Suddenly, somebody screamed from the back, and said, "Ah! I have come to drink blood." And immediately, all the people on the same seat with her disappeared. This kind of incident can only happen where there is prayer. She was quietly seated during the sermon and praise worship sessions, but when we began to throw stones of fire, trouble started.

Prayerlessness is a serious problem requiring violent actions. A person could sit down and pray for five minutes, while another fellow does the same prayer for two hours. And God looks down from heaven and awards the fellows who has prayed for five minutes a pass mark. He would say, yes, this one really prayed.

The Prayer Eagle

But to the other fellow who prayed for two hours, God would say this one is just making noise, orderly noise.

Remember the story of those two in the Bible: One was a tax collector, and the other a pharisee. The Pharisee prayed a very long prayer: 'I thank God I am not like the other men. I pay my tithe and give alms to the poor. I am not like that tax collector over there. But the Bible said that the tax collector did not raise up his head. He had his head bowed, and said, "O Lord, forgive me, I am a sinner." And the Lord looked at both of them and said that this tax collector who prayed in only one sentence has prayed. But the pharisee has not prayed, even though he was sweating, shouting and shaking his head.

The situation was so serious that Psalm 79:6 lamented:

Pour out thy wrath upon the heathen that have not known thee, and upon the kingdoms that have not called upon thy name

The above message is telling us that prayerlessness can make the wrath of God come upon the heads of human beings.

Sometimes ago, I met a very big and influential man in this country, shivering. Why was he shivering? Because he had a copy of a weekly magazine called TELL. He had read from that magazine that people were being killed for rituals. He began to wonder why and how. He used to think it was wild tales as he could not bring himself to believe that even in the civilization, people's heads, breasts and eyes could be severed for rituals. "I used to think they are superstitions. I have been too careless", the man concluded.

This is why I said that those who, hitherto do not pray would soon start praying. A lot of people are going to start praying soon.

A lot of people still come to the place of prayer only to make noise. And they are not getting results because of sin in their lives. The Lord is saying, you are just making a noise, I cannot listen to you. So, God may be saying you are prayerless because the quality and quantity of the prayers you send to heaven have been amputated by sin.

Someone who is praying, suddenly stops the prayers because the fiancee has just walked in: " Hello darling! How are you?" The prayer is thus abandoned, shoved aside, and replaced with chatting. They will both chat until 12:00 midnight before they see-off each other. When the fellow returns, prayer cannot continue as fatigue has set in. May God have mercy on us.

> Isaiah 43:22 But thou hast not called upon me, O Jacob, but thou hast been weary of me, O Israel.

The above passage was a complaint on prayerlessness.

> Jeremiah 10: 25: Pour out thy fury upon the heathen that know thee not, and upon the families that call not on thy name: for they are eaten up Jacob, and devoured him, and consumed him, and have made his habitation desolate.

This is a very serious statement. It means that if a family does not have an altar, God is going to pour out His fury upon such a family. It has been said that a family that prays together stays together, while a prayerless family will always scatter. The Bible says, pour out thy fury upon the heathen that know thee not; and upon the families that call not on thy name.'

Hosea 7:7: They are all hot as an oven, and have devoured their judges; all their kings are fallen: there is none among them that calleth unto me.

This is the lamentation of God about prayerlessness. It was not as if they were not praying at all, but as far as God was concerned, their prayers did not go past the ceiling.

If you do not wage war against and overcome prayerlessness, it can destroy you. That song-writer wrote: " What a friend we have in Jesus; O, what peace we often forfeit; O, what needless pain we bear. All because we do not carry 'everything' to God in prayer,"

The Prayer Eagle

Everything includes the paintings on your toes, lips and fingers, as well as the goat hair you are attaching to your hair; the chain on your neck, marks on your face, the short and tight skirt you are putting on. Everything includes mermaid jewellery and the head-gear you are wearing - take everything to God in prayer. Say, "Father, should I buy." or wear this? And he says "Buy", or Do not buy. Your shirts, shoes, and skirts - take everything to God in prayer.

The degree of your holiness, can be measured by the temperature of your prayer-life. You may tap your foot on the floor like a snake, refuse to shake hands with or talk to a woman, or refuse to eat any food cooked by a woman because you do not want to be polluted, but if you are prayerless you cannot be holy. When the prayer altar is full of ashes instead of fire, the enemy comes in.

When the altar of prayer is full of smoke, you will be battered and bruised. Every spiritual decay begins in the closet. And this decay needs to be checkmated with prayer. All the rottenness will begin to manifest, if not arrested on time. It will appear as if one has cancer in the bone. The person may be walking around, smiling and exchanging greetings with people, but the internal decay has begun. A prayer-less Christian is a powerless Christian.

When we were in the Sunday School class years ago, we were taught some powerful songs. One of them is, "Read your Bible, pray everyday, and you will grow, grow, and grow. Do not read your Bible forget to pray, and you will sink, sink and sink." So when a Christian is prayerless, such a Christian can be tortured and troubled at will by the enemy. That is why we do not deceive anyone here at Mountain of Fire and Miracles. The devil is ready to carry out every church activity but not prayer. The devil was in charge of songs before he lost his throne in heaven- he was the choirmaster of heaven. With him around, you do not need the guitars or drums. If it is preaching, the devil is a good preacher. He knows and can quote the scriptures even better than you and I.

The Prayer Eagle

There was a certain church in Lagos where the elders and members were involved in a very serious quarrel. This quarrel got so much, that one day, while the pastor was delivering the sermon on the pulpit, somebody stood up from the congregation, marched to the pulpit and brought out a powerful juju from his **Agbada** as well as the horn of a ram, and began to rain incantations on the pastor.

After he did this for some minutes, the pastor simply smiled, dipped his hands into his own pocket and brought out much more powerful charms. When the man from the congregation now saw that the pastor had a more powerful charm, he quietly but quickly went back to his seat.

Then the pastor put his own charm back into his pocket and continued with the sermon. The tragedy of this all was that, some people still sat down there listening to the man's sermon. So, you can now see that the devil can also preach.

The Prayer Eagle

One day, the Lord showed me a vision: He said, "Son, this is the kind of thing that would happen in the last days." Suddenly, I saw someone dressed like a pastor jump out from a vehicle in the market place and immediately, began to preach: 'The kingdom of God is at hand; you must all repent now,' And very soon, people gathered around him.

But suddenly, this fellow threw his Bible down and began to tread upon it. With all this going on, he was still preaching. The Lord now told me that these are the kind of things that would be happening in the last days. They would be speaking the word and be trampling on the scriptures.

Prophesying? The devil too can prophesy, In the book of Acts, chapter 16, there was a young girl with a demonic spirit who prophesied. She was following Paul all over the place saying: These are servants of the most High." Perfect information! But Paul knew that she was not speaking by the spirit of God.

THE DEVIL'S WHIMS

Somebody who has just done a one - hour rigorous prayer went to a corner to start brooding again over his/her problems, casting aspersions on God and confessing negative words like, "Ah, when shall I be free from this bondage? " it is just as if that person has not prayed at all. The devil knows that the more we pray, the more miracles will happen in our lives and demons will be ejected. The devil knows that the more we pray, the more strongholds would be pulled down, and the more glory will cover our lives.

Therefore, the devil struggles and fights a lot, so that we do not pray, and has been using the weapon of sin which he knows that God hates with perfect hatred to amputate the lives of many. It is very sad, beloved, when you see very talented brothers and sisters who have the capacity to pray heavens down, but just one little 'pep sin' that they are nursing in their hearts, has converted them from eagle to chickens; it has converted them from prophets to parrots.

The Prayer Eagle

The devil has used the weapon, 'ignorance' to battle prayer lives. He has used the lack of genuine baptism of the Holy Spirit to battle so many to a stand - still. The Bible says we know not how or what we should pray about, but the spirit Himself maketh intercession for us with groanings that cannot be uttered. But some people do copy their tongues from American Television. Some people would copy that of a great man of God. Others would just look at somebody they like and begin to mimic him or her. So the bottom - line is that, a lot of people do not have the genuine baptism of the Holy Spirit.

The devil has used the weapon of laziness, to cause prayerlessness. He has used the weapon of improper Christian foundation, to fight prayer lives. May be right there where you are, you do not know the basics of Christianity - salvation, justification, redemption, and sanctification, then your miracles will not be stable until you have a solid foundation.

The Prayer Eagle

Those who have the foundation of holiness do not know what God has done for them. There are some that do not have that kind of foundation. Their idea of Christianity is the preacher throwing his shoes, jacket and handkerchief at the congregation and everybody struggling to catch them and falling on one another. They fall down as sinners and rise up as same. This is their foundation. They do not understand the basics of Holiness, and this will definitely affect their prayer lives. They therefore need to go back to that foundation.

The devil, has used the weapon of emptiness to cage many prayer lives. He has used the weapon of listening to the enemy to affect the prayer lives of many. He has used demonic bondage to cage the prayer lives of many people. Prayer can be a torture to anyone under demonic bondage.

I gave a sister a prayer point to pray. The first night she started, she said about forty hefty men moved into her bedroom to harass her. They asked her why she went and collected the

The Prayer Eagle

prayer point from "that man'. "Therefore, we shall now go ahead to discipline you." And true to their threat, they beat the day- lights out of her.

After doing this for about an hour, with marks all over her body, they went away, and warned her to desist from continuing with the prayer, while promising to come with full force if she continued.

The next day, the sister continued with the prayer and within one hour, they were back. She was given another serious beating- this happened on a Monday.

On Tuesday, she refused to continued with the prayer point, and that night, had a sound sleep, nobody came to harass or beat her.

By Wednesday, she came to report the incident to me: I said , " Go back to the prayer" But she said, "No, they will kill me O." What is happening?. Nothing but torture. However, I prayed with her and asked her to go - "They will not touch you again." I told her.

FACTORS RESPONSIBLE FOR PRAYERLESSNESS

Sin - God hates sin with perfect hatred. The Bible says, "His ears are not heavy neither are His hands shortened that He cannot hear or save us, but our iniquities have taken Him far away from us."

A praying sinner would not get results; and the Bible says that the prayers of a sinner are an abomination unto God.

Some people get so much worried when their herbalist parents refuse to bless their marriage even though they know it is in a demonic way. But I normally ask them what kind of blessing they expect from a herbalist. Thank God that such parents had even refused to pray, because unto whom are such prayers offered?

Once sin is in the camp, prayerlessness will set in because immediately you say, father in the name of Jesus, satan will say, "Shut up, yesterday, you stole, and remember you are keeping malice with someone, so what are you saying now?"

Except you just want to bombard your conscience and continue, just like a lot of people use noise to bombard their conscience and go home instead of agreeing quickly with the devil.

Ignorance - Ignorance on the why, how, when and where to prayer

Ignorance cause prayerlessness. If it was not ignorance, why should somebody ask you to remove your clothes, climb on top of the Bible and offer prayers? And you obeyed. Why should somebody ask you to stand inside a bucket of water and begin to pray? Or why should you be asked to stand on top of a mortar and pray? Ignorance.

Not receiving genuine baptism of the Holy Spirit

The Bible says, " Likewise the Spirit also helpeth

our infirmities; for we know not what we should pray for as we ought: but the Spirit itself maketh intercession for us with groanings which cannot be uttered." Since it is the spirit that knows the mind of God, it is then the spirit that can frame prayer in a way that will be acceptable to God.

So, without the Holy Spirit, a person would be prayerless or at best, struggling with a few words, or could even purchase a prayer- book. But the devil too can read.

When we give some people prayer points to take home, or they purchase our prayer booklet, they still come back to ask how many times should the prayer points be read.

Some of them would say, "Sir, I read it three times yesterday." That is prayerlessness. When the Holy Spirit is there, and you pick a prayer point, it can take you to the east, west, north, upward and downward, in fact, you could be on that single prayer point for one hour and the Holy Spirit says continue. That is part of the benefit of receiving genuine Holy Spirit, and not the tongue you copied from American video tapes, or the one you learned from one man of God somewhere or by reading a book, or the one you like so much and then copied.

Laziness- The truth is that many Christians are very lazy, especially when it comes to spiritual exercises.

Improper Christian Foundation- A person calls himself a Christian simply because his father was born into the house of a priest, then he has become a Christian. Not that he was born- again, no foundation about holiness, on sanctification and living a good life. Virtually nothing to build upon. Such people will become prayerless.

Emptiness- This refers to those who lack the word of God. They do not know the Bible or what the word of God is saying about their situation. Such people, as far as God is concerned, are empty and will be prayerless.

Listening to the voice of the devil- This causes prayerlessness because the devil does not have any good message for anybody. It is only messages of discouragement, malice and bitterness - in the fact, all forms of bad messages.

When you listen to the voice of the devil, you will not pray, because he will give you a hundred and one reasons why you should not pray, and why prayer would not solve the problem.

Demonic bondage- When somebody is under the bondage of demonic spirits, the fire of prayer in such a person's life wanes. The person would have the internal urge to pray, but would be unable to pray. This confirms the fact that the spirit is willing, but the flesh is weak.

Readers of the Bible would remember that Peter slept about three times. First of all, he slept on the mount of transfiguration, in the place of fire. He also slept in the garden of Gethsemane when he was supposed to be on guard for Jesus.

The Prayer Eagle

Peter slept during the time of tension when he was not supposed to sleep. Again, he slept while he was in jail, but this time, he had already received fire. He was not the old Peter again, but another kind of Peter, that an angel woke up.

Now, if somebody is under any bondage, no matter how powerful the environment is, he or she would still not be able to move. Thus, praying can be a torture to a man who is under demonic bondage.

I remember the testimony of that brother who was very, very demonic. He was so demonic that he had swallowed birds. Then, he got born-again and went for deliverance. But the deliverance minister forgot to deliver him of all the birds he had swallowed. And anytime he prayed and called fire, the birds got agitated in his stomach and began to eat up his intestines.

Gradually they ate up almost a quarter of his intestines, which led to his hospitalisation at the University College Hospital, Ibadan. And at the end of it all, some parts of his intestine were cut off after a major surgery.

TYPES OF PRAYERLESS PEOPLE

In Christendom, we have so many prayerless people, namely:

The prayer collectors- These are people who consume prayers. They cannot pray on their own or listen to sermons, but they keep soliciting for prayers from men of God. They send prayer requests to all the churches around them, both holy and unholy. Even when you advise them against this step, they will tell you that they are only harassing God in order for Him to answer their prayers. Eventually, they would have unconsciously sent prayer letters to their enemies. These people are known as prayer collectors.

When the prayer collectors come to a group meeting, they would only murmur when asked to pray for the church, the country or someone else. But you ask them to pray against household wickedness, they become thunderbolts, and suddenly recover their lost voices.

Even during vigils, these prayer collectors would always present their prayer request in the middle of prayers - they will not wait for the appropriate time.

Prayer killers- These set of people are prayer extinguishers. They do not pray at all. The prayer lives of many sisters who were on fire for the Lord die, immediately they get married. They are married to prayer extinguishers. Many brothers, as well, that had been on fire for God; who used to give God holy attention - they want to pray for just thirty minutes, but God will keep them there for two hours, get married and everything disappears.

Prayer killers are those people who doze off during church services.

In those days, when I was a young Christian, I used to tell the Usher not to wake up

These people pray a lot and still get suffocated at night while sleeping. They get spiritually harassed after violent prayers.

The procrastinators - They always threaten to pray down the heavens, but are unable to perform. They never have the time for serious praying because the enemy has given them assignments that would steal away their time and prayer. They would stay glued to the T.V. and Newspapers - they read and watch and waste time. No prayers.

Even when God says, "Son, daughter, I want to speak to you at 9.00. O'clock" He replies, "Sorry, I want to listen to the 9.00. O' clock news on television." They keep pushing things forward. They make promises that they would do this or that after sometime or later on. They have theoretical zeal but poor finishing - no practicality.

The time wasters- Time wasters fast a lot but do not pray; they shut the man out and would not let God in.

The devil uses gossips, unprofitable discussions, and vagabond thoughts to render them powerless. They live a planless, directionless, purposeless and disorganised prayer life. You are a time waster if you lack concentration or focus and live a planless life.

At this juncture, beloved, pray this prayer-point with holy aggression: "Lord , I want to depart from the school of prayerlessness; I want to ascend the mountain of prayer, in the name of Jesus."

The prayer doves- Their prayer lives have assumed the character of a dove. They scrutinize the prayers of others, while they themselves do not pray. They are the good questioners - always asking about this or that?

They are people who do not like to sweat during prayers. They tend to believe that prayers should not be too hard. They are spiritual gentlemen- gentle and nice to the enemy. They do not understand what is meant when the Bible says that, " As Jesus prayed, the

The Prayer Eagle

sweat dripping down his body was like drops of blood. "They would not understand it because they are doves as far as praying is concerned.

I remember the first time I received the power of the Holy Ghost, it was at a meeting where I was seated at the back.

The first thing that interested me at that meeting was, the preacher and his interpreter. The interpreter had a large protruding stomach that was touching the pew. While the preacher was pacing up and down, his interpreter just stood still at a particular point. I became amused, but in my amusement, the Holy Spirit said to me, " Do not let this amuse you, just listen to what this man is saying".

Eventually, he said we should start praying. But there was a man who sat beside me. From his looks, it was clear that he had just had his bath and had his perfume on. He had powder rubbed all over his face despite the fact that he was a man.

The Prayer Eagle

The first prayer point was called and we started praying. I prayed aggressively. And there was this other woman who somersaulted to our side. But this man just avoided everybody, went to a corner and was gently shaking his head, while muttering words. This man is an example of a prayer dove. Such people do not generally get anywhere.

I was therefore not surprised when a very young girl started confessing that each time prayers were going on, they (witches), usually walked around the arena, looking for those ones who do not pray or who mumble words. She went on to say that such people are given hot slaps across the face.

There is a particular preacher in the Northern part of the country who calls very strong prayer points.

If we do the same thing here which the preacher does, people will call us witches. This is because he is not kind at all with his prayer points. And if you ask him why, he will always describe vividly what an eagle is like.

Prayer of the prayer eagle live longer- We know that the eagle lives longer than the average human being. They live for an average of one hundred and twenty years. Therefore, prayers continue to live, long after prayer-eagle are dead and gone to be with the Lord.

Prayers of the prayer eagle pursue and overtake- We have been told that the eagle can move at about 135 miles per hour. The prayers of a prayer-eagle can pursue and overtake.

Prayers of the prayer eagle can penetrate into the heavenlies- The eagle is called the king of all birds. By the same token, prayer is the battle-key in the mighty conflict.

Now, why is the eagle called the king of the birds? It is because of the amazing height to which it can ascend. It can fly over 30,000 feet above the earth, right into the second heavens where aeroplanes cannot even get to, and where there is no gravity.

The Prayer Eagle

Prayers can go right through to the second heavens, and from there to the third heavens. No wonder the ancient people call the eagle the bird of heaven.

Prayer eagles are kept in the secret place- The eagle builds its nest in the most inaccessible place on top of the rock. It is the same thing with the prayer eagles - they hide there, where nothing shall by any means hurt them.

Prayer eagles see clearly- Off all creatures with feathers, the eagle has the strongnest vision, the sharpest eyes. At 10,000 feet above, the eagle can see a small fish inside the water. The eyes of the eagles are about either times sharper than the eyes of man. It is also the same thing with the prayer eagle. They can see what they will see. They know man for what he is. They can discern and they can see, even though they remain quiet.

For example, there is no place in the Bible where we are told to call people's names: this one and that one are witches. In fact, it is not wise to point them out, just know and leave them alone. Bind the snakes inside of them.

Every pursuer of prayer eagles never succeeds- The Eagle can discern its prey from afar. When it is high up in the air and men cannot even see it, it can see everybody. Not only this, the eagle is the only bird that can look directly at the sun and fly towards it. So, when an enemy is pursuing the eagle, what it does is to locate and fly towards the direction of the scotching sun. Every pursuer of the eagle does not get half way with it because of the heat and rays of the sun.

It is the same thing with the prayer eagles. They are the only ones who can stand before the throne of heaven and come back with shining faces.

Prayer eagles are of power and courage- The eagle is a bird of power and courage. It can seize big animals about five times its own size and carry them away with its claws. Prayer too has nothing to do with your size or age.

The Prayer Eagle

Prayer eagles' lives are renewed- The eagle also renews its youth. Sometimes when its feathers are old and ugly, it sheds them off and puts on new and beautiful feathers. That is why prayer eagles look younger than their age. If you see a person who is a prayer eagle, he looks a lot younger than his age. They retain their vigour even at old age.

Prayer eagles feed on the blood of the enemy- Eagles feed on flesh and blood, they do not eat rubbish. Prayer eagles too are the ones who will drink the blood of the enemy. *(Number 23:24)*

Prayer eagles are burden bearers and intercessors, fresh and energetic- Not only this, the training school for the eagles is very tough, likewise is the prayer school. When the eagle is training its young to fly, it throws them out, and when they are about to hit the ground it catches them again.

The eagle trains its young to be able to look at the sun. Any baby eagle, that is not able to

The Prayer Eagle

look straight at the sun is killed by the mother-eagle. Prayer eagles are not to catch up with when pursued by the enemy. Prayer eagles are always fresh and energetic.

Many people realise that they have a battle to fight, but they find that the power to pray is not there. When you become a prayer eagle, you will be the first to launch the attack - you act first. You do not wait for the devil to take control before you overthrow him. You pray preventive and attacking prayers. You do not have to wait, until your whole business is messed up before you start pleading the blood of Jesus.

Prayer eagles do not beg the devil to leave them alone, they order him to leave and not come near them.

A brother once told me that there was a man in his place of work sometimes ago. He said that once this man arrived in the office every morning, fifteen minutes before the commencement of work, he would close his eyes and pray.

The Prayer Eagle

At break time, when almost everybody must have gone for launch, this man would close his eyes and pray.

Again in the toilet, he does the same thing. He is the only one who would not crack jokes in the staff bus on their way home- always praying.

Then, after a while, he was promoted just after one month in a particular unit within their organisation. This man was promoted again after only a short while in another unit. And this went on like that, just like fire. This is what happens to those who can pray.

Actually, anyone who can pray does not have any problem. But a person would have problems, only if he or she cannot pray.

" To start with, the prayer- warrior may look like a fool, like somebody who does not know what he or she is doing, but will eventually laugh last at the end of it all.

The prayer eagle would do the battle at the

enemy's gate and would not allow it to take place in his house. They would do battle for unseen things, pray about what they cannot see, and cause trouble where they have not even stepped their foot.

These are the kind of things that the Lord wants us to be engaged in.

Now, ask yourself, to which class do you belong, and to which class do you want to belong? Some prayers can scare the whole of hell fire. But the devil does not even notice that some people are praying. Some prayers have no effect on the enemy at all, while some have no fire in them.

The question is this: Where are you now on the ladder? Do you have a weak prayer-altar? Are you a blind, lame, deaf and dumb prayer man or woman?

So many of us would need to increase our prayer tempo, if that break through we desire must come. A lot of us would have to become

The Prayer Eagle

much more serious than we are now, with our prayer lives, if we are ever going to make heaven. You will discover that with the little praying you have been doing the devil is pulling you back and forth. You fall today and say," Oh God, I am sorry", you fall again to more sins and you apologise to God every day. At the end , you console yourself by reading from the book of proverbs which says a righteous man falleth seven times and riseth again.

The question is, when the righteous man is on the floor and the trumpet sounds before he gets up, what will he do? It is therefore better for the righteous man to remain standing.

That was why Paul said, "Let him that thinks he stands, take heed, lest he falls." Sometimes, when people fall, and we complain that they are falling, the problem is that they have never even stood before. It is only when somebody is standing that you can say he has fallen.

SOLUTION

Ask yourself again, to which class do you belong? And what must you do? The first thing to do is this: set a special time aside, privately for this exercise, if you are determined to mount-up with wings as eagle. Right there in your closet, you can call upon the Lord and things will happen. You do not need any man of God to pray for you-just plug yourself into heaven. Yes your Pastor and your General Overseer may give you guidance and counsel you, but at the end of the day, it is just you and God- one to one.

The man of God may pray for you, but if you are an enemy of God, the prayers would not be answered, so set time aside, if you want to become a prayer-eagle.

Read and meditate on the lives of prayer-eagles in the Bible. Daniel and Elijah were human beings, just like myself. What made they strong? What made them prayer eagles? Ask yourself these questions and meditate upon their lives.

Confess and renounce all your sins as you are reading this book.

Purge your life thoroughly with the blood of Jesus.

Forgive all those who have offended you.

Ask for the spirit of supplication and prayer

Supplication and prayer are spirits which can come upon you if you ask for them like this: "Let the spirit of prayer and supplication fall on me, in the name of Jesus." In addition, pray in tongues if you have been baptised with the Holy Spirit.

Ask for the fire of the Holy Spirit to come upon you.

Go into purposeful fasting.

Take authority over the spirit of dryness in prayer.

Pray as you have not prayed in the past.

Intentionally prolong your prayer time.

Ensure you pray for nothing less than half an hour each day.

If you adhere to all the above mentioned, and stick to it with all your heart, a time will come when it will become natural with you.

Now, you are going to pray like a prayer-eagle. You are going to pray the following prayer points, but before then, bow down your head and begin to confess your sins to the Lord. Ask the Lord to forgive you.

If you are reading through this booklet and have not yet given your life to Jesus Christ, then it has to be done now. Please say the following.

"Lord Jesus, I come before you today. Come into my life take control of my life, in Jesus name I pray." Amen.

PRAYER POINTS

1. Every satanic altar, raised against my prayer-life, I pull you down, in the name of Jesus.

2. Every demon of lukewarmness and coldness, get out of my life by fire, in the name of Jesus.

3. I refuse to be a deaf and dumb prayer-warrior. In the name of Jesus.

4. Let every power, chasing blessings away from me, be paralysed, in the name of Jesus.

5. Let the enemy, begin to vomit every good thing he has eaten up in my life, in the name of Jesus.

6. O Lord, give me the power, to overcome every obstacle to my breakthroughs.

7. I break, all curses of leaking blessings, in Jesus name.

8. I clear my goods, from the warehouse of the strongman, in the name of Jesus.

9. Let all satanic kingdom, working against me fail, in the name of Jesus.

10. Let all hidden arrows in my life, be troubled in their hiding places, in the name of Jesus.

11. I frustrate and disappoint, every instrument of the enemy fashioned against me, in the name of Jesus.

12. I disarm, every household enemy today, in Jesus name.

13. Let all those who troubled my Israel, be troubled to death, in the name of Jesus.

14. I scatter, all evil counsellors and conspirators fashioned against me, in the name of Jesus.

The Prayer Eagle

15. I scatter, all evil forces shedding blood on my behalf, in the name of Jesus.

16. O Lord, sharpen my dull sword (not studying the word) and repair my broken shield (doubt and unbelief).

17. I take authority, over every satanic attack on my home, in the name of Jesus.

18. I withdraw the staff of office, of the strongman delegated against me, in the name Jesus.

19. Let every opposition to my breakthrough, crash into pieces, in the name of Jesus.

20. I stand against, every faith destroyer in my life, in the name of Jesus.

21. I stand against, every unprofitable agreement and reconciliation, in the name of Jesus.

22. I refuse, to assist my enemies to fight, in Jesus name.

23. I paralyse, everyone behind the extension and the expansion of my problems, in the name of Jesus.

24. Let every tree of sorrow, be uprooted in my life, in the name of Jesus.

25. Let the rain of fire, fall on the camp of every hardened enemy, in the name of Jesus.

Other Publications By Dr. D. K. Olukoya

1. 20 Marching Orders To Fulfill Your Destiny
2. 30 Things The Anointing Can Do For You
3. 30 Prophetic Arrows From Heaven
4. A-Z of Complete Deliverance
5. Abraham's Children in Bondage
6. Basic Prayer Patterns
7. Be Prepared
8. Bewitchment must die
9. Biblical Principles of Dream Interpretation
10. Born Great, But Tied Down
11. Breaking Bad Habits
12. Breakthrough Prayers For Business Professionals
13. Bringing Down The Power of God
14. Brokenness
15. Can God Trust You?
16. Can God?
17. Command The Morning
18. Connecting to The God of Breakthroughs
19. Consecration Commitment & Loyalty
20. Contending For The Kingdom

21. Criminals In The House Of God
22. Dancers At The Gate of Death
23. Dealing With The Evil Powers Of Your Father's House
24. Dealing With Tropical Demons
25. Dealing With Local Satanic Technology
26. Dealing With Witchcraft Barbers
27. Dealing With Unprofitable Roots
28. Dealing With Hidden Curses
29. Dealing With Destiny Vultures
30. Dealing With Satanic Exchange
31. Dealing With Destiny Thieves
32. Deliverance Of The Head
33. Deliverance: God's Medicine Bottle
34. Deliverance From Spirit Husband And Spirit Wife
35. Deliverance From The Limiting Powers
36. Deliverance From Evil Foundation
37. Deliverance of The Brain
38. Deliverance Of The Conscience
39. Deliverance By Fire

40. Destiny Clinic
41. Destroying Satanic Masks
42. Disgracing Soul Hunters
43. Divine Yellow Card
44. Divine Prescription For Your Total Immunity
45. Divine Military Training
46. Dominion Prosperity
47. Drawers Of Power From The Heavenlies
48. Evil Appetite
49. Evil Umbrella
50. Facing Both Ways
51. Failure In The School Of Prayer
52. Fire For Life's Journey
53. For We Wrestle ...
54. Freedom Indeed
55. Healing Through Prayers
56. Holiness Unto The Lord
57. Holy Fever
58. Holy Cry
59. Hour Of Decision
60. How To Obtain Personal Deliverance
61. How To Pray When Surrounded By The Enemies

62.	I Am Moving Forward
63.	Idols Of The Heart
64.	Igniting Your Inner Fire
65.	Igniting Your Inner Fire
66.	Is This What They Died For?
67.	Kill Your Goliath By Fire
68.	Killing The Serpent of Frustration
69.	Let God Answer By Fire
70.	Let Fire Fall
71.	Limiting God
72.	Lord, Behold Their Threatening
73.	Madness Of The Heart
74.	Making Your Way Through The Traffic Jam Of Life
75.	Meat For Champions
76.	Medicine For Winners
77.	My Burden For The Church
78.	Open Heavens Through Holy Disturbance
79.	Overpowering Witchcraft
80.	Paralysing The Riders And The Horse
81.	Personal Spiritual Check-Up
82.	Possessing The Tongue of Fire

83. Power To Recover Your Birthright
84. Power Against Coffin Spirits
85. Power Against Unclean Spirits
86. Power Against The Mystery of Wickedness
87. Power Against Destiny Quenchers
88. Power Against Dream Criminals
89. Power Against Local Wickedness
90. Power Against Marine Spirits
91. Power Against Spiritual Terrorists
92. Power To Recover Your Lost Glory
93. Power To Disgrace The Oppressors
94. Power Must Change Hands
95. Power To Shut Satanic Doors

BOOK ORDER

Is there any book written by Dr. D. K. Olukoya
(General Overseer MFM Ministries) that you would like to have:

Have you seen his latest books?
To place order for this End-Time materials.
Text your request as follows

* Book title(s)
* Delivery Address
Call: 08161229775

Battle cry ministries...equipping the saint of God
God bless

Made in the USA
Las Vegas, NV
20 February 2024